Gregory A. Hill Publishing Co.

Houston, TX

Printed in the United States

Book Cover Design by

Gregory A. Hill

Email: gahillpublishing@yahoo.com

The Other Lost Boys

The Other Lost Boys

The *OTHER* Lost Boys

Purpose

In the "concrete jungle" of our society today, particularly in our minority communities, it may be fair to say that we are on a road to a type of "apocalypse", referring to a final battle, or the end. The young men that are making up this generation of fathers, and the next, are painting a picture that is very frightening. In fact, it may not be much of a picture at all. A very tiny part of it will be fathers at home, nurturing and raising their children, and the other part will be fathers that are in jail, those who have met unfortunate deaths, or ones who simply were never there at all, physically or emotionally.

My purpose in this writing is to provide some of what I believe to be "overlooked" insight into the psychology of many of our youth today. I believe that most people, teens, as well as adults, are often not fully aware of what drives and shapes some of the most important choices of their lives. The subtle, but powerful influences that control most of our decisions often go completely undetected by the average person.

It seems that too often when we face problems in our country today we focus more on the symptoms than on the cure-that is, if we even admit there is a cure. Not to say that those symptoms don't need to be treated, but too often we look at "pain relief" as a cure, and seldom get to the root of the problem to bring about the real cure. I firmly believe that finding the root of the problem should always be the desired goal. In order to find that "cure", it is vital that the problem is diagnosed properly.

I had a conversation with a friend recently and they were trying to justify their smoking of marijuana by saying that it was no different than any other drug, and therefore should be legal. They were suggesting that it should be on the drug store counter next to the headache pills-besides, "it is considered a natural herb," they said. My comment was that the headache pill, like almost all other drugs, had a purpose of *temporary* pain relief, and they were never intended to be used permanently. So at the very least, if a person is smoking "MJ", there should be plans to stop taking the drug at some point, and work on the source of the pain.

Anyway, back to my point. Searching for a cure usually means looking not only at the obvious, visual things, but also the subtle, quiet, non-visible things that are often the most powerful. Most of the time, when you ask a person why do they favor or prefer a particular thing, the most common answer is, "because that is just what I like." Most never accept or realize that most of those "likes" were results of outside influences, or inner emotional deficiencies which need to be satisfied.

The role models of people, music, advertising and propaganda virtually rule the world. We are all being influenced to some degree by forces we refuse to recognize. Most are completely unaware of, will not believe, or refuse to admit to, the extent of those influences. That is largely because of our inability to self-diagnose, our stubborn pride, our low self-esteem, or the need to appear to be our own person, and in control. Those things refuse to let us believe that we being manipulated in our thinking and decision-making. *We are not in as much control as we think we are.*

My challenge is difficult simply because it deals with the complex brains and emotions we all have, particularly during adolescence. The subtle, and typically the most powerful, influences in our lives are often very difficult for most people to detect, which makes them even more difficult to overcome.

Whenever the topic of poor decision-making comes up, the most common statement is one about choices. Certainly it goes without saying that we basically become an end product of the choices we make. The most common attitude is this: As long as we have the proper information, know the difference between right and wrong, and understand the consequences of our actions, all the things necessary for making wise choices are in place. God gave us all the same ability to choose, and there is no excuse for consistently making poor choices.

Often we see people in circumstances that are seemingly the same as our own. Since *we* made the proper choice, we assert that person "X" was just as capable of making the proper choice also. It reminds me of testimonies we've all heard: "I pulled myself up by my bootstraps and they can do the same." Therefore they deserve little, if any, sympathy, mercy or help. Part of my goal is to challenge, or perhaps, adjust that mindset, if I may.

The Other Lost Boys

To some extent that may be true. It assumes however, that everyone has straps on their boots. In my experiences, I will submit to you that some people do not even have boots.

I chose the fable of Peter Pan and his "Lost Boys" because it provides a good background for comparison of today's youth. It is my hope that after reading this all of us will see that making wise choices involves more than we typically realize-and that life is not 'that simple' for many of us.

In a cruel sort of way, there is an inbred unfairness woven into the fabric of virtually all societies. At a particular age society deems a person an adult, making them and them alone responsible for their actions. Unfortunately, before that age, many, many children experience various types and amounts of severe trauma that was completely beyond their control. Nevertheless, once they reach adulthood they are the ones that must be responsible for managing/overcoming the effects of that trauma. Right or wrong, fair or unfair, that's just the way life is.

Introduction

Most of us are familiar with the fictional characters of Peter Pan and the Lost Boys of Neverland. They live in an imaginary world on an island as boys who will never grow up as long as they continue to live there. Peter Pan is the leader, protector, and role model of this bunch of pre-teen boys. Supposedly these are boys "who fell out of their cribs and wandered off" when the babysitter was looking the other way. If they were not reclaimed in seven days, they were scooped up by a fairy (Tinkerbell) and taken to this place called Neverland." There, Peter Pan and the rest of the boys spend their never-ending childhood adventuring on the small island, interacting with the locals-mermaids, fairies, pirates, etc.

The Lost Boys are typically pictured in rag-tag clothing, living off the land, and having no guidance from any adult figure. They never have the ability or opportunity to travel outside of Neverland, so the island surroundings are all they know, and it's the only place they feel comfortable. Their virtual surroundings, in very subtle and unconscious ways, became their new family, and their new home.

In the version of the story entitled "HOOK", when dinner time comes around there is no visible food on the table. The boys must use their imagination to "conjure" up their meals. You could say they simply "ate off of the land."

The *OTHER* Lost Boys represent modern-day "at risk" kids. We have all heard the term "at risk", and it typically has referred to young men who have gotten themselves in legal trouble, or who appear to be on a fast track to jail. These are ones who grow up in *obvious* bad circumstances. They walk among us, lining the streets of our neighborhoods, leaving the educational system, and limping through life. If they have not already become a part of the juvenile justice system, they are knocking on the door.

However, there is another group. These are the ones who don't "appear" to be at risk. Many of these *Other* Lost Boys have never been in trouble with the law, and likely never will be. Nevertheless, they are locked up in their own personal prison of loneliness, confusion, and a life without direction. If you were to meet them there likely would be nothing readily visible about them that would lead you to think they are at risk. They are, but just in a different way. If you could see their inner emotional turmoil, you would see a different type of dysfunction. They live in a fantasy world where they seem to be happy, but deep inside they, like the other "at risk" kids, are missing some extremely important elements in their lives.

What you are about to read is in no way intended to excuse delinquent and anti-social behavior. Rather, it is an attempt to truly examine and explain it. It is my hope that the light that is shone will help all of us to understand the real problem with our youth so that we as a community can deal with all sides of it with the mercy, compassion, understanding, rehabilitation, and discipline that is appropriate.

The Other Lost Boys

So, take this journey with me to Neverland and when the tour is over, it is my hope that a clearer picture will come into focus of how to address the crisis in our communities. So, fasten your seat belts, fix your eyes, and open the ears of your hearts.

The Daily Routine

It's a family affair:

Perhaps one of the most important things to humans, and most animal cultures, is a sense of, and need for, family. It is the place where we are supposed to get our most vital needs met. There is the physical aspect that includes having adequate food, clothing and shelter.

Perhaps more importantly, family is a place that is supposed to provide a sense of self-esteem, encouragement, acceptance, stability, role models, a foundation of faith and trust, and ultimately, who we are; it is the birthplace of our primary relationships. Family is the first place that we are supposed to be rooted and grounded in this thing called love. Far too many people simply assume that all family members have that because these are elements that often go unseen. Again, those subtle things that can't be seen are often the most powerful forces in our lives.

Family is the primary building block on which we are supposed to build our lives. After family comes many other factors such as relatives, neighbors, teachers, friends, and the community in general. All of these persons and things will play an important role is life's decisions and choices. Nevertheless, the relationship with family is almost always the primary weight that swings the pendulum one way or the other.

It can be compared to a cake recipe. We know that the recipe starts with the most important ingredient, flour. The other important ingredients are things like eggs, sugar, butter, milk, vanilla extract, and various other flavorings. If you mix all of the secondary ingredients together and leave out the flour, your "cake of life" will most assuredly be a mess.

In most cases the people we call family are blood relatives. However, in my life I have come to know that it is not uncommon or inappropriate to deem other people 'family" even though there are no "blood ties." The saying goes like this: blood doesn't make family, love does. At a point in many people's lives there is an emotional connection made with a friend that super-cedes the relationship that normally comes from blood relatives. That can happen in good or bad family relationships.

Even in good family relationships it is not uncommon for someone outside of the family to relate a person in a way that none of the relatives could. There are many times that we consider an "outsider" family simply because we are exchanging those earlier mentioned family traits in a way no blood relative had ever done. The subtle but powerful elements of good family relationships are typically the main force that will affect one's choices.

The Other Lost Boys

Breakfast:

I'm sure most of us have heard by now that the most important meal of the day is breakfast. As far as I understand, it basically has to do with getting a good start to one's day. Since the body is recovering from a "fast' that you did while sleeping, the body needs that "recharge" of energy to get the day started off on a good foot. That good morning start can have a notable influence on the rest of the day.

Back when I was growing up, most days started with a bowl of Kellogg's Corn Flakes, often floating in a bowl of powdered milk. (I'm sure some of you have no idea what powdered milk is). Anyway, as we became more "affluent", we were able to afford *Sugar Frosted* Flakes. Regardless of what the breakfast was, it was something that was ingested on a daily basis and played a significant part in our daily function.

For a period of time during my elementary school days lunch was simply milk and cookies. We would get a nickel for lunch money. It wasn't enough to buy an actual school lunch, but that simply was all that was available. On the way to school, we would stop at the neighborhood store to buy cookies. They were two for a penny, so the nickel would buy ten cookies. Five were eaten on the way to school, adding to a breakfast we may or may not have had at home. The other five were eaten for lunch along with a free, small carton of milk we were given at school.

During the summer, there was always *something* to eat, but it wasn't necessarily called breakfast, lunch, or dinner. It could range from a mayonnaise sandwich to a bag of potato chips. (Yes, that's right. A mayonnaise sandwich is just what you think. No meat, just mayonnaise between two slices of bread). It was often washed down with sweetened water. (For those who don't know, that is sort of like Kool-Aid, but without the flavor-just sugar and water. There were times when we did not have enough money for a package of Kool-Aid.

Just as physical food has an effect on our physical health, so does the daily "emotional" food we ingest affect our mental and emotional health.

In a perfect world, one's emotional breakfast would consist of things like consistency, trust, nurturing conversation, encouragement, reasonable expectations, appropriate discipline, and respect, floating around in the milk of loving and stable relationships. None of those things are ever perfect, and they don't have to be. All in all, this is hopefully served up in a bowl called love. That expression of a love relationship is the source of most of the daily strength we need in order to win the battles between right and wrong choices.

Unfortunately, too many of our adolescents are having to eat a breakfast that mostly consists of instability, disappointment, various forms and levels of abuse, neglect, loneliness, abandonment, and confusion. This all floats quite well in the milk of instability, in a bowl that has no "feeling" of love.

The Other Lost Boys

*

One juvenile that I talked to never really had a sense of home. As far back as he could remember, his address changed four to five times a year. That also meant that his circle of friends usually changed, as well as his educational setting. Staying out late at night, getting high, and sleeping through most of his classes each day were the things he did in order to cope. Those things, along with instability, were about the only things he could count on. The anxiety was evident in the 13- year-olds' hands. He was still sucking his thumb each day until its skin was raw, and his chewed knuckles stood out because it caused discoloration of the brown skin of his hand.

He talked about his absent father who offered no support of any kind. As a result, he was exploring every opportunity available to do whatever he could to try to help the rest of the family. He told me that when he was released, he would likely begin selling drugs in his apartment complex in order to help the family's desperate financial situation. He noted that he watches people in his apartment complex do it every day and they never get caught. He obviously had already learned the "tricks of the trade." He knew that he was too young to get a job, (even though he was quite willing). Though he never asked, I could sense the unspoken question on his mind-"do you have a better suggestion?" I knew that telling him to just 'hang in there' was not an option. There I sat, looking in the eyes of what I am certain was a kid who wanted a regular, law-abiding life, but his unspoken question was one that I had no immediate answer for.

*

The Other Lost Boys

Getting Dressed:

In any version of Peter Pan, the boys are dressed in a rag-tag fashion. Their clothes are typically worn, torn and unwashed. Some parts of their wardrobe never fit properly and going barefoot was just a part of life in Neverland. Their clothing wasn't necessarily what they wanted to wear; it was simply all they had. They rise in the morning from sleeping wherever they can- in a cave, a treehouse, or just somewhere in the woods. (Today it is called "couch surfing"). Their grooming and dress had only two purposes, covering their "necessities", and trying to impress one another-which was one of the main daily activities. The personal validation and sense of self-esteem came from the ones around them-and their "gang leader", Peter Pan.

Fitting in is always the prime objective each and every day. Since these boys never leave the island, the world outside Neverland is only something they heard stories about. On one hand, their neighborhood is cool because everyone in their neighborhood looks and acts like them. On the other hand, violence, poverty and broken relationships have become the accepted norm. In its own way, whether real or not, their environment presented some sense of comfort and security. It was all they had ever known, and as it is with humans, they became comfortable with that.

Their daily wardrobe is topped off by the headbands they wear. It serves as a sweatband during the day and a nightcap when they sleep-it never comes off.

Of course, this headband is part of their emotional wardrobe. It is a headband of rejection. Rejection or flat- out abandonment by father is the one sold in most stores. It is fitting that the aspect of rejection is headgear. The mental reality and confusion brought on by a father that is missing brings with it all kinds of damaging thoughts and emotions.

Island Life:

Most people can somewhat understand how negative elements of the so-called "hood" environment can contribute to bad decision-making. The physical, economic blight is not too difficult to factor in. Often one of the factors that are less understood is the concept of lack of exposure. Though this element may not contribute much to criminal behavior, it certainly comes into play in terms of how the outside world is viewed. It can affect how a person sees their present place in society and their future.

On the island of Neverland, the lost boys had no knowledge of the "outside" world. All of their dreams and goals were defined by the island life itself. To them, that island wasn't just an island, it was their entire world.

I grew up in Atlanta, GA. in the sixties, in a neighborhood that was all African-American. However, it was not just a neighborhood, it was a community. It was the first neighborhood in Atlanta where African-Americans were allowed to own their own homes. Nevertheless, judging by the only standard we knew, itwas a great place to grow up. With a mom-and-pop store up the street, there was never much need to leave the neighborhood. About the only time we did was to go to school, church, or take the bus downtown to shop. Television and those trips were just about our only real exposure to the outside world. (Malls were just starting to come on the scene back then).

One of the things I learned after I went to college was that when a person lives in a "closed" setting like that, not only does it present a skewed view of the outside world, but it also affects how they view the things right around them.

*

Recently I stumbled upon a documentary about severely "at risk" kids in what could be called a typical minority school setting. As it goes, many of the students were dropping out, underachieving, getting into trouble, and so forth and so on. A group of individual school related personnel decided to address the issue from an unusual perspective. It was the birth of an organization called Godparents Youth Organization.

They gathered several of these at risk students, showed concern for them, and challenged them. If the students would improve their academic performance by one letter grade, they would be rewarded with a bus tour across the country the following summer. The idea caught on quickly, and what I would call a "successful family of students" began to emerge. Year after year the buses would be full of students who met the challenge.

Student after student began to give testimonies of how they were inspired by the fact that someone chose to love them, believe in them, and challenge them. The trips around the country opened their eyes to possibilities and potential they had never had reason to consider. Not only did their performance at school improve, but so did their view of life, their view of themselves, and the view of their future possibilities!

At one event during a group dinner, a teacher noticed that one young man, who was a noted gang member, was not eating but was instead crying. When questioned as to what was wrong, here was his response: "I was just overwhelmed because this is the first time I have ever sat at a table and ate with family."

Not only did the young man separate himself from gang activity, he went on to graduate high school and is thriving! What a testimony to the power of love, caring, and relationships.

*

My older sister wrote a book entitled, "The Second Room on the Right". It is an incredible memoir of her interaction inside of our family, while also giving a picture of how our perceptions of the "outside" world were shaped. One of the most notable stories for me was her recall of the events around the assassination of former President John F. Kennedy.

In our world there were only two divisions of society, black and white. From all she could see, it was clear to her that ALL white people were well-to-do financially and had no cares or worries. In fact, even into her teenage years, she could never recall ever seeing a white person cry in real life! (Of course, there wasn't much opportunity to do so).

Well, in November of 1963 that all changed. When President Kennedy was killed, the most surprising thing she noticed was the fact that white people were crying! Since she had never seen that before, it became very clear to her that something very, very terrible must have happened! You see, in our closed neighborhood-our Neverland, we usually didn't concern ourselves too much with outside things-we had no reason to.

For myself, my college degree was in a field that I never knew existed until three months *after* I arrived on campus. I soon learned that many of the things I studied were elements that surrounded me as I grew up, but they were things I never had reason to notice or pay attention to. Things that didn't directly relate to food, clothing, or shelter usually went unnoticed.

At the end of the day, the lack of exposure can lead to underachievement and unfulfilled dreams and purposes. When someone has a calling, or innate ability and no place to channel their gift, it can lead to a shallow, unfulfilled life, and usually the person never knows why. As a result, the decision making process, as well as the choices that are made, are affected.

The Same-yet Different:

It is very obvious to me that too many parents labor under a delusion that is destroying many of our children. Once again, too often we look only at the outside and make judgments that are incorrect. Regardless of who the parents are, each *and every* child possesses a unique

20

personality and makeup that needs to be understood in order to help and allow that child to reach their full potential.

How many times have we heard, or said it ourselves-"God made us all the same- if *that* child did it, then the *other child* can do it, too. Or better yet, I went through the same thing, and if I could handle it, so can they."

What I find so interesting is this. No one denies that people are born with different physical abilities. No one questions the fact that some can naturally run faster, jump higher, sing better, or have more athleticism than the next person. No one questions the fact that some people are more capable mentally than others. I don't mean just the ones who have legitimately labelled mental defects from birth. I include things like math, or physics, etc. Those are all differences we all accept, and can be experienced with our own five senses and physical interactions.

However, when it comes to emotional strengths and weaknesses, many assume that we are given equal strength and capacity in those areas also. It simply is not true. Just as each individual has varying strengths and weakness in physical and mental abilities, those differences also apply to how we each deal with emotional difficulties.

We have obviously made great strides in assisting people with physical handicaps, and make many allowances for people with obvious mental handicaps. However, we seem to be clueless when it comes to traumatic "emotional" handicaps-mostly because they are not easily seen or detected.

Imagine owning two trucks that from the outside appear to be exactly alike. They are both made by the same manufacturer, same color, mirrors, radio, steering wheel covers, and same lights, etc. -all the things a person can see.

Consequently the trucks are driven, used, and maintained in the same manner. Very soon it is apparent that one truck is performing better and lasts longer that the other. One might assume that one simply wasn't put together properly at the factory.

But let's take a closer look at the things that are not so obvious. One truck is a four-wheel drive, the other a two-wheel drive. One has an 8-cylinder engine, the other a 4-cylinder engine. One has steel-belted tires, the other has fiberglass belted tires. And last but not least, one runs on diesel fuel and the other one on regular fuel.

That difference in fuel is the most important difference in the vehicles, but it is the hardest thing to notice! It comes out of the pump, through the hose, and into the vehicle-you never see it. If you put the wrong fuel in the wrong vehicle, it will perform very poorly, if at all.

Expecting these trucks to perform the same under the same conditions is idiocy! They both can do the work of trucks but not exactly the same work, in the same manner, in the same capacity!

Our children are no different. There certainly are similarities, but they are very different in personalities, as well as what motivates and drives them. If there are several children in the home, raised in the same way, it does not mean they will all respond the exact same way to the same stimuli. In fact, it is often a mistake to discipline two different children the exact same way for every offense!

I grew up with a brother that was 2 years older than I. We did virtually everything together, including get into trouble. On those occasions when we got caught the punishment from our father was thorough and extremely harsh. (If fathers whipped their children today the way we got it, serious jail time, or worse, would follow. Nevertheless, it was accepted at that time). Call me a weakling if you like, I don't care. Those few vicious beatings I got were more than enough to keep me out of future trouble. My brother, not so.

Often it took about four days to heal physically, mentally, and emotionally from those beatings. Right about that time, my brother was at it again. For the life of me I could not understand why he would continue to get into trouble, knowing the consequences. It seemed the more beatings he got, the more trouble he got into!

Only when I got well into my adult years did I begin to understand that it is easier and more effective to motivate and guide a child through the proper balance of understanding *and* child-specific discipline, than simply attempting to control behavior only by lecture and punishment. I believe that the biggest challenge parents have is to find out what moves and motivates each particular child. I pray for those with many children like my parents-they had eleven personalities to manage.

So in the end, the stimuli for each individual child must be somewhat in line with their particular personality. Otherwise, the discipline will not have the desired effect. This often creates resentment and emotional confusion, which often leads to that child's flawed decision-making process.

Life Support:

Imagine one day you awake from a slumber and find yourself in a strange and desperate situation. It seems that somehow you have fallen over a cliff and you are hanging there, holding on for dear life. Every time you try to pull yourself up you can't seem to do it. When you look down to see where you are, the surface below is hidden by a cloud-and you don't know where the bottom is. You seem to remember stories of people in that same situation before. Some let go and survived, others let go and they didn't do so well. So, what do you do? If you decide to hang on, how long you can last? If you let go, will you survive the fall?

As our medical technology advances each day, it sometimes brings with it decisions that were not available in times past. In an effort to heal, doctors can now keep people alive for very long periods of time, never being sure if the patient can ever recover. Perhaps the most difficult situation is when a child has a sickness or injury that they may never recover from, and they are being kept alive by artificial means. Once all medical treatments have been done the only thing left to do is to wait. Many times during this process the patient is in some degree of pain. The question then becomes, "how long do you keep them on life support?" Next to having a missing child, it is probably next on the list of parents' worst nightmares.

Unfortunately, many boys are in a similar situation. They are boys who have had limited contact with fathers who are not totally into the father thing-for various reasons. For lack of a better word, some fathers "tease" their sons by sometimes showing up, sometimes not. There are occasional, minor indications that dad wants to be dad, but it never blossoms. Many times there is limited communication with the father, but no real relationship.

The son desperately wants that connection but is not sure if the father does. If he takes the chance and reaches out and gets rejected, he is afraid that the pain may be unbearable. If the son cuts ties and gives up, the same pain may await him. The son, much like the sick child's parents, is hoping that one day dad will truly be a consistent part of his life, despite the many

disappointments. The son is so desperate for dad's love and attention that he will "wait at his bedside", so to speak, until dad "comes around." So each day, the haunting questions are, "will today be the day, or how much longer can I do this?"

So, when does the boy give up on his dad? The reality is that the boy himself is on life support. His emotions force him to try to decide which pain is worse, giving up on dad too soon, or waiting for something that will never come? The son realizes that he may lose with either choice. He may have to "pull his own plug." So, emotionally, the son wanders through the wilderness of Neverland, hanging on to the cliff, can't pull up, afraid to let go. As with the parent, the worst fear is to give up, then find out that if they had held on for just one more day, there would be a happy ending.

As the son goes about his daily business the uncertainty affects nearly every area of his life and brings uncertainty to many daily, as well as lifelong decisions. Such is the situation many adolescents face today with dad. Without that direction from a father, the son is rarely sure which direction to go and how to get there. Even when he makes a decision without that fatherly guidance and support, often the necessary drive and determination necessary to accomplish the goals are missing. Either of the choices, stay, go, or stay in limbo, will affect many important life decisions.

Another somewhat common problem comes when parents get divorced and mom gets custody of her teen-age son. Sometime later mom gets married to a really neat guy that is willing to finish raising the son as his own. One problem though. Although the teen may get along with the new step-dad, he wants to live with his biological father whom he has a strong bond with. Now what?

While on one hand most moms would never consider "turning over their sons", she realizes that if she doesn't, the resentment may tear the household apart. The disappointed, hurt, and angry son now has a powerful emotional war going on that is likely to affect some very important choices in his life. (I actually met a woman in that situation and she recognized the impending chaos. She allowed her son to go live with his father and she got visitation rights. She told me it was the wisest thing she had ever done. Since then all sides have been at peace and her son is flourishing).

A "Seventh" Sense?

Unfortunately, we live in a time where terrorism and mass killings are becoming all too common. In an effort to prevent some of this, there is a certain technology being tested that attempts to actually detect peoples' good or bad disposition/intentions by an electronic scanner. Science and psychology have determined that when we are highly emotional, stressed or traumatized, it is nearly impossible for it not to be shown in some way in our outward behavior. Here is the typical scenario.

At the concert being held at a stadium tomorrow there is expected to be a crowd of nearly 50,000 people in attendance. At each entrance is a "tunnel" that resembles the carriage of an 18-wheeler that each person must walk through in order to enter the stadium. Inside the tunnel is an electronic scanner that reads each person's "body language". It can detect and analyze things such as heartbeat, facial expressions, and various other subtle signals that give a clue to the person's mindset. Most of these "clues" are simply impossible to detect otherwise. The scanner will instantly use the data to determine if any particular person has criminal intentions or not. Basically this device is an electronic profiler. Although it is still being tested, it is very likely that soon it will be deemed trustworthy enough to pass all legal obstacles and be put to use.

Although we all do it, the reading of body language is not a "perfect science", and is subject to our own experiences and abilities. Nevertheless it is often a useful and important part of how we interact with each other. It can be considered an "extra sense."

In our world we are guided in almost everything we do by our five senses: sight, touch, taste, smell, and sound. Those senses alert us to what is real or not real, whether something is good or bad, safe or dangerous. Somewhere, at some time in our lives we are confronted with directions and decisions that can't be determined by our five senses. It is that unknown area that we all wish was more accessible and tangible.

In 1999 the famed movie producer M. Night Shyamalan produced a movie entitled, "The Sixth Sense." It was a sci-fi mystery thriller about a young boy who had the ability, (a sixth sense), to "see into the supernatural." (If you have not seen the movie, what I am about to say will spoil it for you. Perhaps you may want to stop reading and go see it before you continue. If not, well, read on).

He alone could see the spirits of dead people walking around aimlessly, who were trapped between this world and the next. It seemed as though they wanted help to move on but they couldn't get it because no one could see them, in order to help them. They were walking around in society, *in plain sight*, but they were invisible, except to this one boy. The boy's famous line from the movie was, "I see dead people, but they don't know they are dead-and they are everywhere." This obviously caused the boy some psychological problems.

The Other Lost Boys

Actor Bruce Willis had the lead role, giving the boy some much needed psychiatric help. It wasn't until the end of the movie that Bruce himself realized the he was also one of those "walking dead people." (He was shot at the beginning of the movie but the audience was "led to believe" he survived).

Apparently when a person is "stuck between two worlds", their existence is filled with uncertainty, fear, anguish, frustration, and confusion. They seem to be searching for their place in this world but nothing or nowhere seems to be right. Though they aren't dead, they somehow don't feel completely alive either. In many ways they often feel like society's "misfits."

One of the strongest desires that we possess is the need to feel like we belong, or fit into the society, or at least the neighborhood. That need is one of the leading factors that get people into trouble- especially teenagers! In teenagers, the need to "fit in" is second only to the need to eat and breathe...sometimes.

One of the reasons some adolescents feel like misfits is that they feel invisible. Just as the "dead" people in the movie, they were longing to be noticed and recognized. The feelings of emptiness and lack of direction that come from not feeling recognized and valued can be devastating, reaching to the category of trauma.

Back during the time when I grew up there was a common saying that all children learned early on. It went something like this: "children are to be seen and not heard." Now, in the proper context, there is much validity in that s t a t e m e n t . I believe that its intent was good, but it often brought about an unintended result. I believe it was intended to teach children to be respectful, and not to attempt to indulge into adult's matters and conversations in inappropriate times and places.

As we get into our adolescent years, we all have the need to be heard, to have someone listen to us, and accept the thoughts, ideas, dreams, and inadequacies we feel, without judgment. That is one of the most important elements of feeling loved and important. It helps give our lives substance and meaning. (Self-esteem) We all have a need to be accepted just for who we are. That is something we need to feel early on, as children. When that element is missing, it often results in feelings of loneliness, rejection, and invisibility-much like the dead people in the movie.

As I have seen many examples of this over the past several years, it seems that I too, have developed an extra "sense", as it were. The feelings of loneliness, the pain of rejection, the confusion, lack of direction, and lack of identity will begin to show themselves over time outwardly in the lives of young men, and women. I can usually detect that in many cases after a five minute conversation I can sense that there is/was no notable or healthy male role mode in their lives. Sometimes I can tell simply by the way they carry themselves- even just by watching them walk down the street!

Remember, as I said from the beginning, I'm not talking just about juveniles and "bad kids." These *Other* lost boys are what we label as "good" boys. They may be sitting next to you in church, or good, well-mannered students in school. Nevertheless, these, as well as the troubled kids we all hear about, are all 'lost boys', and often they don't even know they are lost! I see them everywhere.

Though many times they have managed to stay out of trouble, be assets to society, and often go on the college, typically their achievements and accomplishments fall far short of their potential. If one can look past the false "make-up' of things these boys do to fit in or cope, one would see many of the ingredients that make them citizens of the "new" Neverland.

The Trauma Behind the Tragedy

For those who may not know, there is a method to the madness of dysfunctional or delinquent behavior. It is a madness that is usually the result of some form of trauma. In the psychological community the general definition of trauma is "the result of extraordinary stressful events that shatter your sense of security, making you feel helpless and vulnerable in a dangerous world." Additionally, any situation that leaves a person feeling overwhelmed and alone, even if there is no physical abuse, can be a source of trauma.

Individually, trauma is a person's own subjective experience of the event.

Here is what one survey revealed:

Many people experience harsh events in their childhood. 63% of the people who participated in a study had experienced at least one category of childhood trauma. Over 20% experienced 3 or more categories of trauma that fall under the category of Adverse Childhood Experiences (ACEs) listed below:

11% emotional abuse

28% physical abuse

21% sexual abuse

15% emotional neglect

10% physical neglect

13% witnessed their mothers being treated violently

27% grew up with someone in the household using alcohol or drugs

19% grew up with a mentally ill household member

23% lost a parent due to separation or divorce.

5% grew up with a household member in prison or jail.

(Many have lived several of these experiences at the same time)

The outcomes from these traumas are directly tied to the increases in teenage pregnancy, depression, crime, hallucinations, and numerous post-traumatic stress disorders.

I can tell you without hesitation that the numbers are much, much higher in the minority communities in virtually every category. If you add in the "simple" trauma of children growing up without a positive father figure in the home, the numbers and effects are off the chart.

So here we are, proclaiming that the average person's brain doesn't reach a normal level of maturity until their mid- twenties. Nevertheless, we punish their juvenile activities before they can even sort out the past or present trauma. To make matters worse, they simply are not getting the help and assistance needed to rise above it. Simply locking them up doesn't do it. Ever wonder why the repeat offenders are so common?

Most people think of trauma as always being something that is outwardly huge and catastrophic. In reality it can be something seemingly as simple as not feeling loved, or not getting enough attention. Whatever the trauma, to one person it may be a minor trauma, to the other one it might as well be a nuclear holocaust. Every individual handles trauma in their own way, in different degrees.

*

While working with 'Paul', a 14-year-old juvenile at a detention center, he was recounting the details of one of his crimes in which he decided to hit the victim in the face with his gun. When he finished talking I calmly, and without judgment, asked him, "why would you hit someone in the face with a gun?"

His demeanor immediately changed, shown by the somber expression on his face. After a brief moment of contemplation and reflection on the incident his countenance dropped. It seemed as if this was the first time he had even considered his motive. He dropped his head, and in a very sobering voice said, "'because somebody hit me in the face with a gun." There was no doubt in my mind that this was the first time he had ever made the connection between what had happened to him-and his decision to pass that pain on to another.

*

Perhaps one of the most telling examples of how complicated emotional issues can be is the disease of Munchausen Syndrome by Proxy. It is a perfect example of how difficult it can be to understand how a person's choices and actions are linked to childhood trauma.

Munchausen Syndrome by Proxy is where an adult caregiver makes a child sick by either fabricating symptoms or actually causing harm to the child, whereby convincing not only the child but others, including medical providers, that their child is sick.

Some conditions or symptoms that may be faked by the caregiver or parent include failure to thrive, allergies, asthma, vomiting, diarrhea, seizures and infections. These symptoms are easy to fake because when a child goes into the doctor's office, the adult can just say that his or her child is experiencing these symptoms. This usually occurs during the preschool years.

Many experts feel this form of ill-treatment is driven not only by the attention that the child and parent/caregiver receives because of the diagnostic tests that must be run, but also the satisfaction of being able to deceive individuals that they are more important than the victim.

Munchausen by Proxy can have many long term effects on a child. In some cases the child goes on to develop Munchausen Syndrome themselves, which is where they are likely to inflict injury upon themselves or fake illnesses. One reason for this is that they seek the attention they received when they were in poor health. They may also inflict injury or sickness upon themselves so that their caregiver/parent will not leave them.

The Silent Killer

With all of the senseless killings in our communities around the country, with gun violence seemingly leading the way, there is a lot of talk about restricting access to guns as a way to curb the problem. First of all, I am not one who thinks that getting guns off the streets is the real answer. Secondly, I don't believe that it is even realistic-at least not by passing laws for that purpose. But more importantly, the access to guns is in reality a symptom, not the real problem.

Restricting gun laws serves only to address a symptom; not physical ones but emotional ones-hopelessness, anger, frustration, and often a real or perceived injustice. It is simply one of the "faces" of a much larger problem.

Again, we spend countless hours and an untold amount of money on the obvious issues with very little success, issues that for the most part are signs of a larger problem. In the end, we totally miss the real root of the problem. Drug companies make billions of dollars pumping us with drugs that almost never cure anything. As a people, as long as we can get something to "fix" the immediate symptom, we often forget about an actual cure. And almost without fail, the problem resurfaces later, in an equally, and often more dangerous form or fashion, affectionately known to us as "side effects." In society today most of our physical medical issues are a result of two things: poor diets and poor, or non-existent exercise habits. One that we have decided to give a special name to describes the ailment's character. This disease, or should I say ailment, is called high blood pressure.

Many people suffer extreme, and sometimes permanent physical problems because of it and many even die. The main reason is that a person can have high blood pressure and not even know it. That is because nearly all of the symptoms never show themselves outwardly until much damage is done. We all see some of these people every day, and we never have a clue as to what is going on inside. Therefore, high blood pressure has been labeled "the silent killer." Many people go about their daily lives feeding this deadly disease that is slowly killing them and they don't even realize it.

There is another silent killer on the loose that is just as subtle and just as deadly. However, this one is not of the physical nature, but an emotional one. It factors into virtually every decision we make. It tells us what to wear and how to wear it, how to talk, who to spend our time with, what our goals are (or even whether to have any). It has a direct effect on who we choose to date, or marry. It tells us what direction in life to pursue, or sometimes whether to go on living at all. This silent killer is called "poor self-esteem."

In the bible, it is stated that Jesus performed so many good deeds that if they were all written down there would not be a library in the world that could house all of the books. In my opinion, trying to chart the numerous effects of poor self-esteem would also fill an untold amount of books. The silent killer of low self-esteem in its own way can be more deadly than high blood pressure.

A person's self-esteem is supposed to start at home, first with the parents, followed by extended family. If not found there, the next place that is looked to is outside the home. The "false" self-esteem that is available in the streets is better than none at all. Enter the phase of "fitting in", and that is normally with a not-so-good crowd.

In a real irony of life, a mirror can be both the best and the worst thing for a person, depending on perspective. On the one hand, when a person looks in a mirror, they may look at themselves as miracles of creation. However, if *they* don't like what they see, it can be an experience of trauma and depression. It doesn't take long for a child to learn that we are first judged by the way we look-then how we act. Those are the first two elements that teens attempt to adjust in order to fit in.

The deception is in thinking that everyone else sees you the same way you see yourself. The truth is, the way you look *and* sound to other people is different than how *you* think you look and sound. The majority of us don't think we measure up. Because after the visual comes the judgment of *the rest of you.* The desire to fit in and make a good impression is so strong that we immediately begin to determine if we measure up to our peers. We attempt to highlight areas that we don't like and downplay areas we think are less attractive.

If necessary, we will adorn ourselves physically and emotionally with clothes and false pretenses that *we* think will make us more desirable to the group. Rest assured, we will get some type of self-esteem from some source... a good one or a bad one.

Now back to the subject of choices. Three of the major priorities of the human brain are survival, security, and comfort. That applies to the physical *and* the emotional area of one's life. We can easily relate to and understand those three areas in regard to one's physical well-being. However, I believe few have a good grasp of how that translates to a person's emotional well-being. Rest assured, our emotional health is as much a factor in our decision-making as is anything else. In fact, when major trauma is at the door, it usually becomes the leading factor.

Of all of the incredible things that our brains do, one of the most important features is how it acts as our "security system." We are designed to survive, and whenever that survival is threatened, physically or emotionally, our brains shift into another gear-and priorities change. In essence, when we feel threatened in any way, our brain begins to bring our safety or survival instincts to the "front of the class." Many times, those instincts push aside rules and consequences, particularly when our pride or pain convinces us that if we "do the wrong thing the smart way", we can avoid the consequences. That is especially true for adolescents.

If the situation is desperate enough, our survival instincts typically take over and virtually control all choices that we make as it relates to our present, or on- going, trauma. When in survival mode our main focus is on surviving that *moment or situation*. What may happen next week or next year is reduced in importance accordingly. In desperate times, the mental and emotional states function on a mindset of "if I don't take care of today, there may be no next week, or next year." The end result is that we look for the fastest and easiest way out, and therefore become short-sighted in our decision making.

- Starvation Mode -

It is my understanding that as human beings, we begin to starve after approximately 40 days without food. At that point, the body literally begins to eat itself. Remember, the brain is the body's ultimate survival tool, and it will shift into whatever gear it deems necessary to keep the body alive.

Question: How many days will you go without food before you will go downtown, in the middle of the day, and eat out of the trash can, without regard to who sees you, or who bit off the food first, not caring if it is diseased?

Every single one of us has that breaking point, and I feel safe in saying that only a very few of us will make it to forty days. (One person told me they would probably break down at day three.) Even though some may consider this an extreme example, it is a daily reality for many. At some point, everything that you are and have ever been taught goes out the window when your only priority is food-any kind, from anywhere. There is no thought or fear of the consequences because your brain will override what you once considered normal, right, and reasonable thoughts and decisions. Your new reality is this; if I don't eat today, there will be not tomorrow. That is trauma at its peak.

That same process takes place when we are emotionally traumatized. Just as your brain will come to the rescue in times of physical distress, it will do the same in the face of severe emotional trauma. Your decision-making process has a new priority.

- -

Nearly everyone experiences some form or degree of trauma. **My assertion is that the strength to make good decisions in the midst of severe emotional trauma comes mostly from the condition of the primary relationships that "should" be in our lives. The love and acceptance that comes from stable parental, family, and community relationships has the ability to provide the strength one needs to balance the trauma that is at the door. I believe that it is the very foundation and origin of the strength that one needs in order to manage difficult decisions- c h o o s i n g the easy way out, or the "right" way out.**

Good, solid relationships can be compared to the deep underground foundations of tall buildings that are unseen, and never thought about by most people. When storms reach hurricane force, the part of the 40-story building that we can see is not what keeps the building from blowing over. Rather, it is the solid relationship it has with the underground foundation that keeps it upright. No matter how beautiful and stately that building appears to be from the sidewalk, if the "unseen" foundation is not in good shape, it may not weather the storm. A person's self-esteem is t h e b u l k of that foundation.

I am reminded of a statement made by a young man who was a successful college football player who talked about his behavior while away at school. He said, "for the most part, I didn't do a lot of crazy (bad) things when I was away from home because I did not want to damage the **relationships**, or bring shame to, the family back home that loved me."

As mentioned in my previous book, "My Father, This side of Heaven," I am convinced that a person's primary source of self-esteem was originally intended to be the father, then the mother. The self-esteem that needs to be nurtured in each child covers many areas that are too numerous to count, and most of them are very, very subtle. If you have ever seen a diagram of the network of complex neurons that make up the human brain, it is a good picture of the complex nature of a person's self- esteem and emotional makeup. Obviously I can only touch on a few of those areas, but each area has a profound impact on our lives, and our decision making.

The father's encouragement, unconditional love, support, hugs of affection, (that's huge, by the way), respect for the son's aspirations and dreams, rendering of fair and appropriate discipline, and showing respect and affection for mom, are vital to the son's self-esteem. That is just the tip of the iceberg, as it were. Of course, for any of that to take root, the father needs to first of all be there.

The *Silence* Killer

On the emotional side, when we are saddened or traumatized, the emotional pain is as dangerous to our mental health as infected blood is to our physical health. That emotional pain needs to be "drained" in order to eliminate the emotional poison that comes from the trauma. Crying is often a critical part of the process to drain that emotional poison. The other "treatment" that needs to take place is simply talking about it. That often means exposing an uncomfortable and/or embarrassing area of ones' life. Many victims decided early on to never relive that shame or pain. As a result, the poison never gets out, the pain never stops, and decision making becomes twisted.

In a sense, the pain becomes pre-emanate, which means the pain is now in charge. Therefore, if severely traumatized long enough, your choices now are subject to whatever eases your pain, with little or no regard to what's right or wrong, or what the consequences may be down the road.

Unfortunately, most boys are taught early on, usually by some male, that a major quality in being a man means never showing weakness. Number one on that list is "no crying." Very early in life boys are taught that tears mean you are weak, and men are supposed to be strong. Tears and "emotional stuff" is for the women only. The death of a loved one is about the only time a boy is "allowed" to cry, otherwise, he is likely to be "cursed with the label of "sissy", regarded as soft, and faces not being accepted into the group. Unfortunately, as he goes through life, there likely will be several scenarios where not only is crying appropriate, but necessary.

Here is the comparison. (I learned this from the old cowboy movies I watched as a kid, so if I'm a little off, you'll understand). If a person was bitten by a poisonous snake, the first thing that must be done is to drain out the poison before it gets in the bloodstream. (Back then it called for actually biting and sucking the poison with your mouth). Otherwise, the infection will spread and cause much more harm, sometimes even death. And so it is with emotional poison.

In a real sense, crying is one of the body's "natural" healing drugs. For that matter it is more like a natural cure. Refusing to cry is like taking an "artificial" drug. And as with nearly all artificial drugs, there are usually significant side effects. In this case, one of the side effects of not crying is that it will cause severe emotional dysfunction somewhere else that could last a lifetime.

This refusal to show weakness rears its ugly head upon entering parenthood, if not before. In dealing with past emotional or traumatic issues, denial becomes a normal way of life. In an effort to shun any sign of weakness many walk the path of false strength and pride. Men particularly become masters of holding in true feelings and pretending everything is okay. Much energy is used to "push down" the inner turmoil, and many convince themselves that they are okay. Eventually, that too, becomes "normal". As a result, they go through life with an emotional limp that has become normal to them. They have convinced themselves that they are "walking through life" normally.

With subtlety being the potent force that it is, one of its biggest and most effective weapons is ironically, silence. So many times it is the things people don't say that becomes the most lethal poison in their soul. The shame, embarrassment, fear, and even the thought of reliving extremely traumatic events are simply too difficult to face.

In addition to that, often the silence is rooted in a fear of how a person may be viewed if they expose certain shameful events in their life-to anyone. Even if it were something embarrassingly horrible that was done to them, (i.e. rape), there is a fear of being looked down upon, or simply looked at, differently. That applies to men and women.

We all have our personal coping mechanisms to try and convince ourselves that nothing is wrong. It gives us a way to walk through life hiding our past (or present) hurts from ourselves. Most of us find something in our personality to hide behind, using it as a shield to distract us from our inner reality. Drugs, sex, and alcohol are the outward ones. Most of the emotional ones are much more subtle, but serve the same purpose. In almost every case, the beginning of the healing process starts when a person finds *someone* that they can trust with their life, and tell their story.

The bible encourages us to bear one another's burdens. It is just short of a miracle how effective that is. The reality is that unless someone *really* knows you, the good, the bad, the ugly, and the painful, you are carrying that pain a l l by yourself. In virtually every case it creates the feeling of being all alone in the world. Though some may tell you that they prefer it that way they are deceiving themselves. Their loneliness and avoidance of relationships, is nothing more than an "emotional drug". It is a drug that keeps you from being hurt, again. You have decided that the pain of loneliness is better than risking another devastating relationship. Being alone is not how we were made to be.

Rarely does simply sharing your life story bring about a solution, but what is does is allows someone else to come into your world. And when you allow someone to "come into your world", it literally cuts the weight of your emotional burden in half, so that you can bear it, and help position you to make better decisions.

Understand, it never has to be broadcast or made public. Simply knowing that one person understands, that is all that is needed to begin to overcome the trauma, heal the pain, and begin to make life livable.

There are some instances where people hide their pain and refuse to share certain traumatic experiences because of the damage it is likely to do to others. Often painful, devastating secrets are kept locked away because "exposing the enemy" would also destroy, or negatively affect other people, or their reputation. That's a call each person has to make. Regardless of the reason, remaining silent creates the perfect breeding ground for the continued effects of emotional trauma-the trauma that creates fertile ground for bad choices and bad decisions.

The Other Lost Boys

Though outwardly they appear to be fine, well-adjusted individuals, inwardly their low self-esteem is covered by the clothes from a lost boy's closet. Just like the boys, I can see their rag-tag emotional attire –but they will forcefully deny its' existence. (Remember, if I can see "emotionally dead" people, I can see t h e i r rag-tag clothing).

Perhaps my favorite movie of all time is "Antoine Fisher". Beyond any doubt it is the one that I have watched the most. It is the movie that was very inspirational in what I do. For me, one of the most telling scenes was when he gave his example of continued disappointment, and how it affected him. In describing how constant disappointment took its toll on him and his decision making, he used the example of rainy days.

He noted that children want to, and need to, play outside. However, when it rains and playing outside becomes a no-no, it is disappointing and depressing. Nevertheless, even children come to accept that those occasions are a part of life. On the other hand, if it rains too much, that state of constant disappointment takes a devastating toll on a child's attitude and outlook. Eventually, the hope of ever playing outside again is locked away in an emotional chest. It soon becomes easier and less painful to give up the thought of ever playing outside again. It is as though the weatherman doesn't care if I play outside. Translation: "because dad keeps disappointing me, I guess he doesn't care either. I must not be important enough."

The Other Lost Boys

Likewise, it speaks to that all too familiar scene of the boy sitting outside on the steps waiting for his dad to pick him up, but he doesn't show up- again. It won't be long before the boy will no longer wait for his dad to come; he simply can't bear another disappointment. The trauma of a life of constant and continual disappointments will affect many important life decisions. Those decisions are likely to include, but not be limited to faith, hope, love, marriage, friendships, security, and the biggie… self-esteem.

Faith, Hope, and Love

There is a bible verse that tells us of the power and relationship of these three words. They are words that are really the key to life, whether a person is a bible believer or not. These are not just bible words; they are real life words, no matter who you are or what you believe.

The simple fact is that no one can navigate this world without faith in something or someone. By simply living on this earth our life hinges on many day to day actions and decisions that require faith and trust. By definition, the only thing anyone really, truly knows is what can be detected by the five senses. For instance, I know that I am sitting in a chair because I can see, feel, and touch it. I don't need faith for that. On the other hand, I am sitting in a building that could collapse around me and kill me within a matter of seconds.

Through experience, I TRUST that such a thing will not happen, simply because of evidence. There are things we do every day that put our lives at risk, and each one rides on the invisible rail of faith. As I ride public transportation I have no way of KNOWING that the driver won't have a fatal wreck, could fall asleep or be suicidal or homicidal-I simply decided to trust. I could fill the next ten pages with absolutely undeniable examples of how every one of us uses life or death faith many times every day.

Whether we want to admit it or not, faith is a key part of our decision–making process. And when it comes to faith in people and relationships, it perhaps is even more important. All true and meaningful relationships are based on faith. That faith is based on a collection of evidence over time and association. As human beings, the core of who we are and how we function starts with the primary relationships in our lives. Those relationships are as important to our decision-making as a steering wheel is to a car.

We all know that no relationships are perfect. Fortunately for us as humans, they don't have to be in order to be effective. Nevertheless, when they are functional, they are the springboard for hope. Hope is essentially an ultimate goal. There are many areas of hope in each person's life. Whether our life is shattered in pieces, or on easy street, there is, or must be, something hoped for, something to achieve. Otherwise there is really no point to life, no reason to go on. (Might that be a clue as to why many rich people who have run out of things to buy and places to go and things to do…end up suicidal).

Hope is kept alive as we see progress and success along the path of life. When at seemingly every turn, over a long period of time, a person's aspirations, plans and expectations are thwarted, it is human nature to begin to think that life will always be that way. Depending on personality, time, circumstance and emotional support, a person can lose hope of life ever getting better. That is a dangerous place to be.

Without hope, there is little reason or incentive to make certain plans. Without hope, faith is no longer a factor. Tangible, factual elements provide the only boundaries for your actions. Without hope, short term thinking is all a person needs. Without hope, life's goals will usually change for the worse, or simply go away. Without hope, the care one has for others, or themselves begins to fade. Without hope, true, meaningful relationships are no longer a part of your value system.

It is virtually impossible to make many good decisions with an eroded value system.

I remember mentoring a young man in prison who had about reached that point. He told me that he had lost hope in ever living a "normal" life, and being close to believing that he could ever amount to anything at all. At the moment, my mission changed. I had to find a way to help him restore hope. I knew that if he could not find a way to hope again, all of my efforts to assist him would be useless. When a person has lost hope, their decision-making process will be affected accordingly.

This thing called love. Of all things discussed, it is in my opinion the most powerful, and in its own way, the most subtle. It dominates every element of our lives. It is the ultimate food for the soul. It is at the very core of our emotional need. It is appropriately associated with the heart, and rightly so. If our hearts don't function at a certain capacity we cannot physically survive. Without the element of love, we cannot survive emotionally. Love is to the soul as physical food is to the body.

The Other Lost Boys

When sufficient love is absent, there is an emotional starvation that begins to take place that has no equal. The feelings of being unneeded, unwanted, unnoticed, underappreciated, unheard, misunderstood, and feeling essentially invisible, will lead to emotional scurvy. (A severe lack of vitamin C in the diet, causing certain physical abnormalities).

In "love starvation mode", we will do things to satisfy our emotional hunger that was once appalling to us. Our brains will allow us to "participate" in actions when we are starving that we would dare not do on an emotional "full stomach."

*

A couple of years ago, Oprah aired a TV panel discussion about the plight of today's youth. One of the panelists made a statement that would startle 99 percent of us. Though his organization's primary focus is education, he counsels students from all walks of life. Here is his testimony: "I have talked to and counseled dozens upon dozens of gang members. He said that every single gang member he has talked to finally came to the point of admitting that the 'real' reason they joined the gang was that it provided a feeling of being loved! It was the only place they had access to where they felt a sense of family. Most of them never really wanted to be in a gang. The need to feel love and acceptance was so great that they simply felt that they had no other viable option.

The Other Lost Boys

Emotional starvation and acceptance is no different. Just as we will eat artificial food when in physical starvation mode, so too, will we consume artificial love and acceptance when facing emotional starvation. Now our decision process has a new, powerful, driving force.

Two Deaths in One

1.Forgive: To grant pardon for or remission of (an offense, debt, etc.); absolve. 2. To give up all claim on account of; remit (a debt, obligation, etc.). 3. To grant pardon to (a person). 4. To cease to feel resentment against: While not forgetting what happened but treating them as though it never did-whether or not they ask for it, acknowledge it or apologize.

Of all the things you have read up until now, this, for many, will be the hardest to swallow. However, I believe that it is the most important. All of us, and or someone we love, at some point have suffered wrong at the hands of another human being. We all know the horrible and unspeakable things that one person can do to another. Often times those events are followed by the words, "I'll never forgive - as long as I live."

While from a human standpoint that is understandable, that attitude will create a self-inflicted, emotional wound that will become the second "silent killer"-in a way more deadly than the first one I mentioned.

At the very core of our human nature lives a supreme need for fairness and justice. When we become subjected to "traumatic and tremendous injustice," it digs a hole in our soul that is virtually a bottomless pit. We are born with a sense of expectation of having certain emotional and physical needs met. As we grow up, we come to believe and expect in our inner beings that we deserve to be loved, nurtured and cared for, both mentally, emotionally, and physically. It is simply a part of our human makeup. When something horrible or unfair (from our perspective), happens to a person, one of the most common statements made are along the lines of "that person did not deserve that."

As young children, when someone hits us, our first reaction is to hit them back. If something is wrongfully taken from us, we desperately strive to get it back. Often, if we can't get it from the thief, we will get it from someone else, giving us a false sense of justice.

When someone has wronged us or hurt us we often feel that we will be forever humiliated, and sometimes even less of a person, if we somehow don't even the score. Until we do, our life feels out of balance emotionally. The torment of allowing someone to "get away with it" grates our very soul.

As life would have it, many times it is impossible to get justice from the person that wronged you. In some cases it may not be particular person, but a system. To make matters worse, sometimes the actual victim is called a liar and can be wrongly painted as the criminal!

Many times the crime or offense committed on a person can leave them in a place of low self-esteem, drowning in a sea of unworthiness. That often leads to living a daily dose of anger, hopelessness, and confusion. Often the faith in a person or a system that was supposed to protect them has turned against them. In our mind, the only way to climb out of our emotional pit is to find some form of justice.

Sometimes we can be satisfied with the "partial" justice that comes when someone simply apologizes. However, when the person who wronged us has died, we still often vex our souls, desperately seeking an apology that is likely to never come.

Growing up there was a saying I often heard to describe people who were so stubborn and defiant that they wanted to get their way even if they came out the loser. Those people would "cut off their nose to spite their face", as it were. Their defiant passion to right a wrong was so important that they did not mind suffering a greater, long-term tragedy just to feel a form of justice, however false it may be. The opportunity to inflict pain on that person and receive a sense of justice was so necessary that it did not matter what it may cost them.

We have all heard of people experiencing some type of physical pain so intense that it affected their mind to the point where they could not think straight, rest at night, and make good decisions. In my previous book, "My Father, This Side of Heaven", I told a story of a woman who had a physical ailment that kept her in tremendous, excruciating, unbearable pain virtually twenty-four hours a day. After the doctors had tried everything they knew without success, they offered her one last desperate treatment.

They told her they could perform a cordotomy on her spinal column and "disconnect" all of her nerve endings, and the pain would then stop. Of course in doing so, it would mean that she would never again be able to feel ANY pain, of any kind, and the process, once done, could never be reversed. The obvious downside to the procedure was noting that pain is a necessary part of how we function because it tells us that something is wrong.

Once the surgery is done, she could cut or burn her arm and would not feel it. When her body sends pain signals that vital organs need attention, she would not even know it. Many people suffer from emotional pain so intense that they decide to have an "emotional" cordotomy. They push the pain down so far inside and they begin to believe and function as though it was not there.

Wallowing in unforgiveness can be viewed as a different form of drug addiction. They both have the same purpose, temporary relief of the pain. They both are very addictive. Becoming addicted to hard and dangerous drugs (even though addictions can be undone), can be just as deadly and dangerous as the cordotomy. As I mentioned before, drugs rarely cure anything, they just provide an outward illusion of health. Meanwhile the longer a person stays on drugs, be it 'cocaine' or "unforgiveness", the severe damage being done on the inside will only get worse.

With either or both addictions, (for they often go hand-in hand), life's danger signs are blurred, warning voices are muffled, and as a result, these "addicts" almost lose their ability to make good choices.

Here is the reality from a biblical standpoint:

First of all, we feel we did not deserve the offense that we, or our loved one, were subjected to. Secondly, we look at ourselves as less of an offender and are better than they are because our sins were "less" than theirs.

Therefore, our souls are burdened with an emotional hole that seemingly can never be filled. The feelings of anger and betrayal trick us into believing that we are somehow getting justice. It is one of the most deceptive and dangerous spirits that Satan tricks us with. It seems to twist our reality into thinking that we are hurting the other person. To whatever extent that may be true, you can bet the bank that much more "life' damage is being done to ourselves.

However, that grudge can have much more severe consequences that can last through eternity. While from a human standpoint holding a grudge is understandable, with God it simply won't fly. In our humanness, we "rate" sins in terms of effect and consequences. (In our earthly society there is some validity for that, just as there is for the different levels of punishment of those sins).

Jesus demonstrated this in the story of the woman at the well. She had committed adultery, and the entire town knew it.

Here is the reality of forgiveness: As your knowledge of and relationship with God grows, you will begin to see sin and forgiveness the way God sees it. The closer you get to that, the easier it will be to forgive. Once you began to get a small sniff of what Jesus endured to cleanse you of your sin, it will be impossible for you to hold a grudge against anyone, for **any** reason. In the meantime it is important to know that if you don't forgive you have condemned yourself.

Here's why. In the Kingdom of God, or in the spirit realm, things are a bit different. In a sense, God cannot "dwell in the presence" of ANY sin, no matter how small or large WE think it is. Even though there are scriptures that seem to indicate that God hates some sins more than others, He cannot dwell in the presence of any.

The parable that comes to mind is in Matthew chapter 18, known as the parable of the unjust steward. In the story, the king rules everything, including having authority over all debt and banking activities.

The time came for one of his subjects to pay his past due bill of "several million dollars" as it were. When brought before the king, the man kneeled, begged and cried for mercy because he could not afford to pay. It meant that he and his entire family could be thrown into "debtors prison" until the entire amount was paid. After some contemplation the king, out of a compassionate heart, decided to show mercy and forgive ALL of the man's debt, and he was free to go.

A few days later, that same man confronted a neighbor who owed him two dollars. This neighbor himself had fallen on hard times and was unable to pay. He too, fell on his knees and begged for mercy. He was given none and was thrown into debtors' prison, along with his family.

A few days later the king heard about this and called in the debtor he had forgiven. The king said, "Didn't I forgive you last week for millions of dollars simply because you asked me to?" How can you be so evil as to not forgive your neighbor of such a small amount? For this you and your entire family will spend the rest of your days in prison.

Here is the key to the story-each of us must figure out which character in the story we are! One of the most difficult things we all must do is to realize that our sin against God........................NO MATTER HOW SMALL WE THINK IT IS- is thousands of times worse than ANYTHING someone can do to us! We can never justify in the sight of God holding any unforgiveness toward anyone...ever, for anything. The scriptures clearly state that if we refuse to forgive others, God cannot forgive us.

When you live a life of unforgiveness there is a darkness that continuously hangs over you. There is rarely any sincere enjoyment of anything. You cannot live life to the fullest. Though you are physically still alive, your daily walk, consciously or unconsciously, puts you in zombie status.

IN TERMS OF RIGHTEOUSNESS IN THE SIGHT OF GOD, ALL SIN IS THE SAME! One person Raped and murdered, and another stole a candy bar. In the presence of God, there can be NO sin. When someone comes to an understanding of who God is and what Jesus has done on the cross, and still hold on to unforgiveness, they basically spit in God's face!

Therefore, from a spiritual perspective, you have put yourself in a place where YOU cannot be forgiven and you may lose your soul in eternity. That is the ultimate second death.

Finally, allow me to paint for you the picture in my mind that may clear things up a bit. When the crucifixion of Jesus is portrayed, seemingly all or most of the focus is on His physical suffering: The nails in His hands and feet, the crown of thorns, the piercing in His side, the beard plucked out of his face, etc. There He hung for hours, thirsty, disgraced, and in a physical pain most of us will never know. While I believe that every bit of that was true, I submit that the "real" pain is rarely talked about.

On the cross all of the sins of mankind, past, present, and future, (something none of us can imagine or understand), were transferred to Jesus. We as humans are not able to comprehend the magnitude of that. That put Jesus in a place where God had to turn His back on His own son! When the weight of that sin took Jesus to Hell, He was literally separated from God for a moment in time! You and I will likely never know, and probably could never comprehend what that was like.

It is obvious Jesus had already imagined it because I believe in His mind He came to a glimpse of it in the Garden of Gethsemane with His disciples. Think about it-Jesus knew what was coming long before mankind had sinned. He agreed to pay that price long before that day. But when the time came and the reality of what Jesus had to do sunk in, His humanity reared its head, and for those moments in the garden even Jesus began to question what He had agreed to do! Not once, but three times did Jesus ask God was there any other way to forgive and save man? When the reality of being separated for His father, if only for a moment hit Him, the humanity of Jesus wanted to back out! The horror He was about to endure was so strong that in a way it made even Jesus question God!

I believe that only when we step into eternity will we be able to somewhat comprehend what it cost God to forgive us as He watched His son die. **No matter what one has experienced on this earth**, (say that a thousand times), it will never even begin to compare to the horror and pain that I believe Jesus endured because of unimaginable love for mankind.

One final note about unforgiveness. When a person carries unforgiveness in their heart, thinking they are somehow punishing the guilty party, they actually add a personal, self-inflicted trauma on themselves! Carrying the "trauma" of unforgiveness doubles the damage that the initial trauma started.

Earlier, I talked about the putting away of pride,

and what one feels they deserve, in order to walk in true forgiveness. Basically what that means is that not only does one give up on the aspect of getting even, in doing so, in a sense, one has to humble themselves to the very person they wanted revenge against! That is why it is so difficult. If one can get past that difficult hurdle, I can assure you that the reward will be worth it many times over.

In a real sense, that is exactly what God had to do. For God, in the person of Jesus Christ, had to step out of his deity, and "lower" himself to human flesh, in order to save us.

*

If you have lived long enough, you have heard of scenarios where two siblings endured the same immense trauma by way of parental actions. One managed to forgive his parents and lived a fruitful life. The other one never gained the desire, or strength to forgive, and led a bitter, unfruitful, and dead-end life. What made the difference was seemingly as simple as a choice. It may never be known what made one sibling let go of the grudge, and the other one to hold on to it. It could have been as simple as the willingness, or opportunity, to talk about it.

*

It is my belief that many who have suffered unimaginable tragedies in this life must diligently seek a relationship with God in order to begin to see everything from His perspective. For many, that will be the only way to find the power and will to forgive. If not, the grudges and unforgiveness will most assuredly ruin this life, and even more likely the one to come-the eternal one.

There are thousands of testimonies of people who tell of the tremendous feeling of relief, emotional healing, and peace they felt after exercising forgiveness. It is only then do people really understand the destructive and poisonous power they had inflicted upon themselves and those they love by holding on to the bitterness and anger.

*

Recently I ran across an article that really spoke to power of forgiveness. It was a typical family with two teenage sons. At some point the mother began to be obsessed with money and things, so much so that she killed her husband for the insurance money. Being a "novice" criminal she was easily found out, convicted, and received the death penalty. Naturally all of the family members drank the bitterness of that for years.

After about 20 or so years, one of the sons found it in his heart not only to forgive her, but successfully fought the impending death sentence and eventually secured her release.

Afterward the son was quoted as saying how forgiving her was the best thing he had ever done. He said that had he known how much forgiving his mother would have changed his life for the better, he would have done it years ago. Living with that bitterness was literally ruining his own life. Now he has a peace that he cannot explain.

*

The Other Lost Boys

At the end of it all, we must remember that Jesus was completely innocent, and he took the pains of all our sins with Him on Calvary. He is the only person who has a right to hold a grudge-yes, even those of us who think they are perfect. But because of His love, He chose not to.

Remember, the bible tells us that there are three things we need to survive. The first two are faith and hope-"…but the greatest of these is love."

What's Next?

*

Recently I heard a radio campaign from an evangelical organization seeking support for a preaching opportunity to a remote village overseas. It happened to be a place of economic drought and hunger was a major problem in the area. The call for funds made it clear that a major part of their work would be addressing the hunger issue. They realized that although the message of the gospel was priority one, they also knew that the growling of empty stomachs was likely to drown out the message they were trying to deliver. So, step one was to fill the stomachs, then their ears would be open to hear the message.

Here is the moral of the story. When people, (especially young people), are emotionally traumatized, it is likely to be very difficult to expect them to take in and use the great advice, direction, and counseling they get from many good, well-meaning programs. Often they are so completely "consumed" by the turmoil in their soul it is extremely difficult to focus on "distant matters". No wonder why so many times good advice, directions and counseling, seemingly falls on deaf ears.

*

In a real sense, mentoring, at its very core, can be nothing more than providing a listening, non-judgmental, sympathetic and understanding ear. It doesn't take months of training and courses. It can be as simple as being a friend who simply knows how, and is willing to, listen.

Hopefully by now I have made my central point very clear. In most cases, the root cause of many of our poor decisions, particularly when they continue to mount up, stems from personal trauma. Trauma, be it past or present, has torn down or completely eliminated basic relationships. As many of us know, sometimes the original relationship that was supposed to be there will never be restored.

It seems that our communities are now flooded with treatment centers in an effort to deal with some of the trauma that is now being recognized. Unfortunately, in my opinion, those centers are most effective on older, more mature people who recognize their destructive behaviors and decide to seek help. Unless ordered by a court or doctor, that group is usually made up of adults.

When it comes to adolescents it is a different matter.

I believe that mentoring is one of the most effective avenues to achieve that necessary relationship. Every mentoring relationship is unique in its own way, and the depth, quality and length of them will vary greatly. A few will be long-lasting, and the involvement can come to feel like family. Some will be short-lived. Most will be somewhere in the middle. Yet, mentoring can be an important first step in the healing and restoration process.

I suspect that you are holding your breath, waiting for some extraordinary revelation, or miracle cure for the ills of today's adolescents. Well exhale, you just read it. Yep, that was it. As mentioned earlier, the simplicity of proper diet and exercise habits, not drugs, are center stage in dealing with most of our health problems. So too, goes the simplicity of dealing with a society of dysfunctional youth. The proper emotional diet, which can start with a mentor, is often the first vital step in curing what ails today's youth.

Society offers many types of self-help and educational classes ranging from anger management to domestic violence. While I am sure that some people are helped by these courses, I still believe in the old saying, "what you do speaks so loudly that I can't hear what you say."

Allow me to translate: what is modeled in front of us is the most effective teacher of all. That is where we are supposed to learn true life and relationship skills. Come to think of it, that is exactly how we *do* learn. The things we learn as children from the "role models" of family, relatives, community *and* society that raised us has deep roots, and those roots are not easily uprooted-be they good or bad.

Since I've never taken any of those classes I just spoke about I must refrain from being too critical. However, I can't help but wonder how often they actually get to the root of the problem. Usually just trimming the fruit from a bad tree relieves the immediate eyesore, but in many cases the bad fruit will return next season. In most cases, the entire tree needs to be uprooted and replanted.

The Other Lost Boys

If I may, allow me to present to you one more analogy. Sitting below a large dam, about one-half mile away, is a typical, small community. One day there is a break in the dam and the water follows its natural path down to subdivision 'A" of the town. Quickly the residents pile up sandbags and diverts the water to save their neighborhood from the dangerous flood waters.

Well lo and behold, what do you know? Now adjacent subdivision 'B" is now suffering the same fate- from the same diverted waters. (I think it is called a side-effect).

Subdivision "B" did what subdivision "A" did. Now I hope I don't have to tell you what happened to adjacent subdivision "C".

My question is, "when is someone going to realize that the dam needs fixing?"

The New Neverland

There is a scripture in the Book of Psalms that states, "The glory of children is their father." I believe it speaks to the way we were created, with our earthly father to be our covering, our guide, our comforter, our strength, and our security. When that is missing from a boy's life his world can literally be turned upside down. From my experiences, when that glory is missing, the path to a healthy, fulfilling life becomes darkened, dangerous, and confusing. It leads instead to a door of a place I call, you guessed it, the New Neverland.

Unfortunately, this new Neverland is growing right in our midst, but this one is very real. It is an emotional island that is being populated at an enormous rate. The lost boys, both categories, are filing in in droves. The boys who are able to dodge death's door will grow older. They will join the other adults that live there. Perhaps the legacy of this Neverland will be the things that these boys *never* attained.

In this new Neverland:

Most boys will never have a good relationship with their father.

Some will never know who their father is.

A few will wish they had never known their father.

Many will never get the answer as to why.

70

The Other Lost Boys

Most will never come close to reaching their full potential.

Many will never trust again.

Most will never know what a loving household is like.

Most will never know what good self-esteem feels like.

Many will never be a good father to their children.

Many will never escape some form of prison-be it physical or emotional.

Most will never attend a four-year college.

Most will never realize that they became the same monster (of a father) that they hated.

And without effective intervention, most will never break the cycle of producing the next generation of Neverland children. But in this Neverland, all of the boys *will* get older... but they will never grow up.

In conclusion, I too, love the stories about the successful ones who have pulled themselves up by their bootstraps. Their testimonies are uplifting and encouraging to the human spirit. Triumph over tragedy; from the muck and mire of life to a mansion; all a part of the human experience.

For me, it may be that I have looked into the eyes and souls of so many young men and have seen their emptiness and their desperation that I am biased and off-center in my reasoning. Maybe I have seen too many wearied and desperate mothers watching their sons slipping away into the darkness of *today's* Neverland- a place from which they may never return, and s h e is helpless to save them.

Maybe I've heard too many stories of boys watching their mothers' "lover" drag her down the street by her hair-

Maybe I am stilled stunned by a story a boy told of watching his mother being raped by her boyfriend-again-

Maybe I've heard too many stories of children
having to move every three months-

Maybe I've seen too many boys with holes in
their souls the shape of their father-

      In the end, some who read this may still stand in judgment of those who continuously make bad choices. Those bad choices are simply the drugs they use to cope with their emotional pain, never willing, or being able to get to the real cure. So if you are one of those taking countless, harmful drugs to ease your physical ailments, rather than change your lifestyle and get to the real cure, perhaps you are violating the same principle.

…And we make the Children Pay

So at the end of it all, we look at the flooded juvenile facilities and see institutions that separate children from society for their bad behavior. But I see something else. In the bible, God speaks of the coming punishment on heathen, ungodly nations that amounts to a form of "generational curses." It proclaims that the sins of the fathers are passed on to their children, through the third and fourth generations". Somehow it seems we are living out that principle in today's society.

In my estimation well over seventy-five percent of family dysfunction is directly tied to the father, and it is very clear that the children are left paying the price, or "holding the bag", as it were.

Whether done purposely, innocently, or ignorantly, it seems that in too many cases we are punishing the wrong people. As mentioned before, on one hand we have declared that h u m a n s d o n ' t develop clear reasoning skills until their mid- twenties. On the other hand, when c h i l d r e n /young adults endure severe emotional trauma in early childhood that results in anti-social behavior, we further advance their dilemma by forcing drugs into their minds and bodies, and locking them away. The reality is that all they did was have a natural, "maturity-related", self -preservation-based reaction to the pain and trauma inflicted upon them.

The Other Lost Boys

So...

-when a parent forces their young child into prostitution
-we make the children pay.

-when the teenage boy has to break the law in order to stop the suffering at the hands of an alcoholic and abusive father-we make the children pay.

-when a mother "allows" her boyfriend to sleep with her child in order to keep him-we make the children pay.

-when a child commits a crime in reaction to the trauma of their parents' sex change and are forced to accept it- we make the children pay.

-and on, and on, and on...

But the children have nothing to pay with- except their hopes, their dreams, their futures, and sometimes their lives- to the third and fourth generations.

Since we all enjoy the stories of rags-to- riches let's make sure we do our part to help them along. To those who want to see more stories of people pulling themselves up by their boot straps, maybe we should consider doing what we can to ensure that these young men at least have boots. And if it's not too much trouble, try to find ones that have straps.

Epilogue

As I think of all the young adults I have encountered, it is extremely disheartening to see that most of them have given up on ever having a meaningful relationship, especially this thing called marriage. All that most of them have ever had modeled in front of them was relationships full of distrust, cheating, lying, and selfishness. They have come to believe that true, loving, lifetime relationships are simply a pipe dream. They live a life of one sexual encounter after another-believing that it is the best they can hope for.

So if you are a young adult, or an old one for that matter, please give your most serious consideration to what I am about to say. As unfair as your life may seem, you owe it to yourself and anyone else you love to not give up on finding a relationship of faith, hope, and love. Those things must be in place for you to have the meaningful life you deserve.

And again, in most cases, it all starts with forgiveness. Once the forgiveness is in play, the seeds of faith, hope, and love can take root. If you take the other route…

*

Many years ago I saw a horrifying tale from The Twilight Zone (I think), about a convicted thief that was sentenced to life for a 10 million dollar heist, although the money was never found.

The Other Lost Boys

After a few years he made friends with the jail janitor as part of an escape plan. The convict had some medical experience and was able to secretly mix some chemicals that would put him in a comatose state such that everyone would assume that he was dead.

The convict was aware of how they handled inmates who died in prison. He knew that the next day he would be put in a pine box and taken outside the prison gates to be buried. He knew that he would awake from the coma about 36 hours later. He plotted with the janitor to split the hidden money if he would help him escape.

The night after the prisoner's death, the janitor was to secretly put a little food, water and a flashlight in his coffin, which he did. At the appointed time after the burial, the janitor was supposed to sneak out at midnight, dig him up, and they both would vanish and split the money.

In a most evil, but perhaps fitting, twist of fate, the next day the janitor suddenly had a heart attack and died. The prison warden decided that the most efficient thing to do was to bury the lowly janitor in the same box with the prisoner who had just died the previous day.

Needless to say, the convict awoke 36 hours later, feeling unexpectedly crowded. He then turned on his flashlight to the most horrifying reality he could imagine.

*

Here is the moral of the story. When you don't forgive, you just might share a spiritual, eternal grave with the one person that you hated, the one you decided not to forgive.

The Other Lost Boys

A Writer's Lament

Who will cry for the little Boy?
By **Antwone Fisher** (With the author's adaptation)

Who will cry for the little *L*ost boy,
Who's lost and all alone?
Who will cry for the little *Lost* boy,
Abandoned, without his own?

Who will cry for the little *Lost* boy,
Who cried himself to sleep?
Who will cry for the little *Lost* boy,
Who never had for keeps?

Who will cry for the little *Lost* boy,
Who walked the burning sand?
Who will cry for the little *Lost* boy,
The boy inside the man?

Who will cry for the little *Lost* boy,
Who knows well hurt and pain?
Who will cry for the little *Lost* boy,
Who died, and died again?

Who will cry for the little *Lost* boy,
A good boy he tried to be?
Who will cry for the little *Lost* boy,
Who cries inside of me?

(I will... I always do).

www.ingramcontent.com/pod-product-compliance
Lightning Source LLC
Chambersburg PA
CBHW022346290526
45786CB00014B/2516